Greenhaven World History Progra

GENERAL EDITORS

Malcolm Yapp
Margaret Killingray
Edmund O'Connor

Cover design by Gary Rees

ISBN 0-89908-019-7 Paper Edition
ISBN 0-89908-044-8 Library Edition

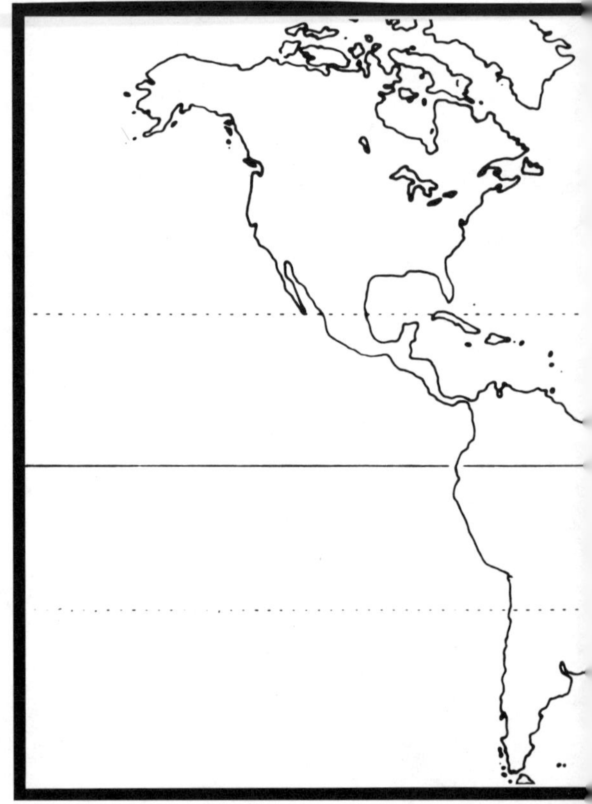

First published in Great Britain 1974 by
GEORGE G. HARRAP & CO. LTD.

NAPOLEON

by Richard Tames

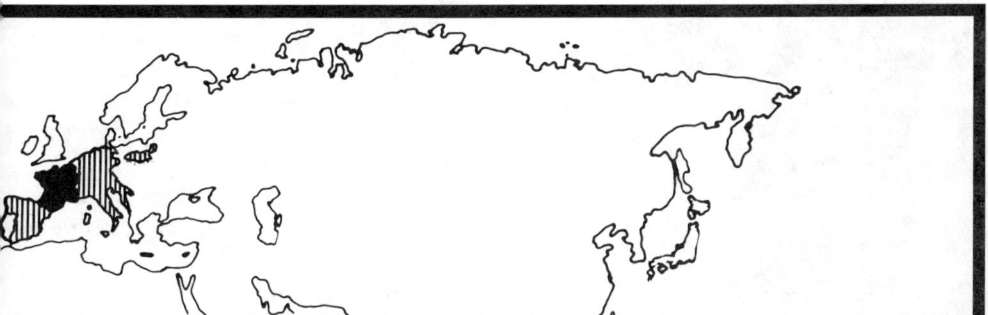

FRANCE

NAPOLEON'S EMPIRE

Greenhaven Press, Inc.
577 SHOREVIEW PARK ROAD
ST. PAUL, MN 55112

A gunner of the French artillery 1790-1815

NAPOLEON, THE GENERAL: FIGHTING FOR FRANCE.

Napoleon was born in 1769, the second son of the poor, proud, noble family of Bonaparte. His home was Corsica, a Mediterranean island which had recently come under French rule. Napoleon was a clever boy and won a scholarship to a military school in France. The other students there teased him because he was not French, but his teachers thought he was a very good pupil. His final report said: 'Constitution and health excellent; character: obedient, amenable, honest and grateful; conduct: perfectly regular; he has throughout distinguished himself by his steady work in mathematics. He knows his history and geography quite well. Fencing and dancing very poor.'

In 1784 Napoleon completed the three year course at military college in a single year and at the age of sixteen became a lieutenant in the *artillery,* the part of the army in charge of the cannon and other large guns.

The French Revolution began in 1789 and the young Lieutenant Bonaparte supported it from the start. He saw that it could open up new opportunities for clever men like himself. Army officers were lucky. Many of the rich and noble officers fled abroad when France became a republic. The outbreak of war between France and other European powers led to the growth of the French army, so that able officers who stayed loyal to the republic had many chances of promotion.

In battle Napoleon showed that he was a brave and brilliant soldier. He went to Paris, the centre of the revolution. At that time France was ruled by a committee called the Directory. Napoleon helped one of the Directors by using his guns against a crowd of demonstrators. Three hundred people were killed. Soon afterwards Napoleon was made general and given command of the Army in Italy. He was twenty-seven.

In 1796 the Directory planned to defeat its enemies by attacking the strongest, Austria. It was planned to make the main thrust directly at the Austrian capital. Napoleon's poorly-equipped force of 40,000 men was to confuse the Austrians by invading their lands in Italy. As it happened matters worked out quite differently. The main French armies were defeated, while Napoleon went from victory to victory. (D1)* Ignoring the instructions of the Directory, he personally made a peace settlement with Austria, which gave France land and other benefits. Napoleon showed that he could be as tough and clever a diplomat as he was a general.

Napoleon became the hero of France. The Directory was unpopular, but Napoleon's popularity kept them in power. The Directors feared that Napoleon might take power away from them for himself. They were glad therefore when he decided to lead an expedition to Egypt in 1798. (D2) Napoleon planned to capture Egypt and thus stop Britain's trade in the eastern Mediterranean and cut her link with her empire in India.

Napoleon smashed the power of the rulers of Egypt at the Battle of the Pyramids. (D3) Then disaster struck. Nelson, the English admiral, destroyed the French fleet. The French army was cut off without transport. Napoleon marched his men north into Syria but was stopped at Acre. He then turned back to Egypt and took ship for France, leaving the survivors of his army behind.

When Napoleon returned to France he found that the Directory

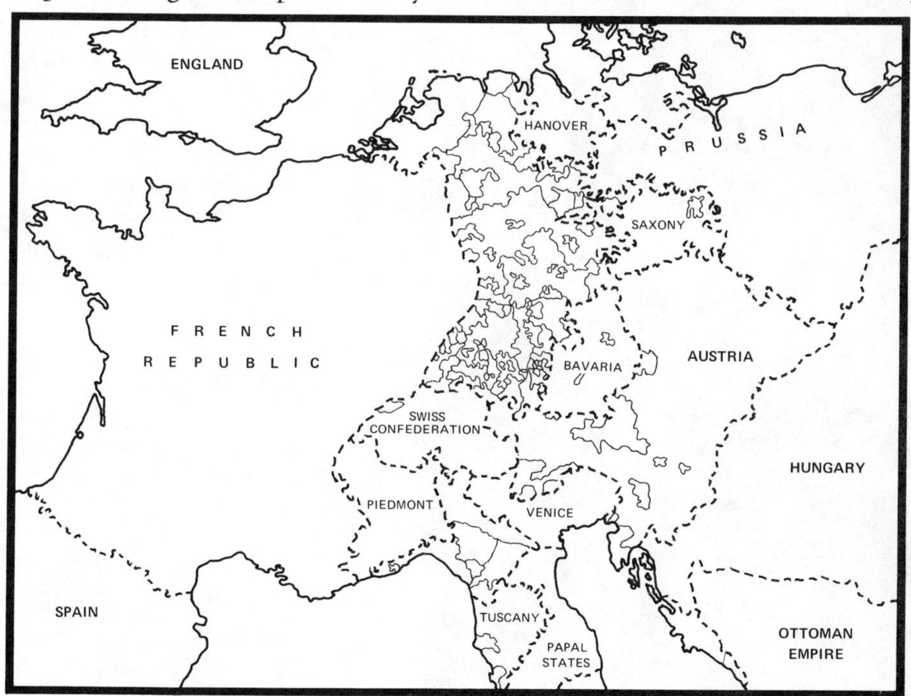

Europe in 1785. Modern Germany and Italy were then made up of a large number of separate states

*The reference (D) indicates the numbered documents at the end of this book.

The Battle of the Pyramids – 1798

Napoleon as First Consul. Napoleon was thirty at this time

was still weak and unpopular. Ranged against France were new, powerful allies made up of Britain, Austria, Sweden, the Ottoman Empire and Russia. One of the Directors decided that the Directory should be overthrown by force and replaced by a strong government able to carry on the war. He thought that the popular young General Bonaparte would make an ideal *figurehead* for the new government. He wanted Napoleon to be a leader without any power, but Napoleon wanted the power for himself, and within a year the same Director told the Senate, 'Gentlemen, you have got a master and a man who knows everything, wants everything and can do everything.' (D4–5)

NAPOLEON THE CONSUL: MODERNIZING FRANCE

The system of government then set up was called the *Consulate.*

Napoleon crossing the Alps. This painting shows a very romantic view of Napoleon. In fact, he crossed the Alps on a mule.

Originally there were three Consuls but within a short time Napoleon was so powerful that the other two did not matter. The French people supported him because they wanted a strong government which would bring order back to the streets and win the war.

In war the First Consul, Napoleon, was brilliantly successful. Austria was beaten and forced to make peace. The French border was extended to the Rhine and states like Holland and Switzerland became dependent on France. With Austrian support

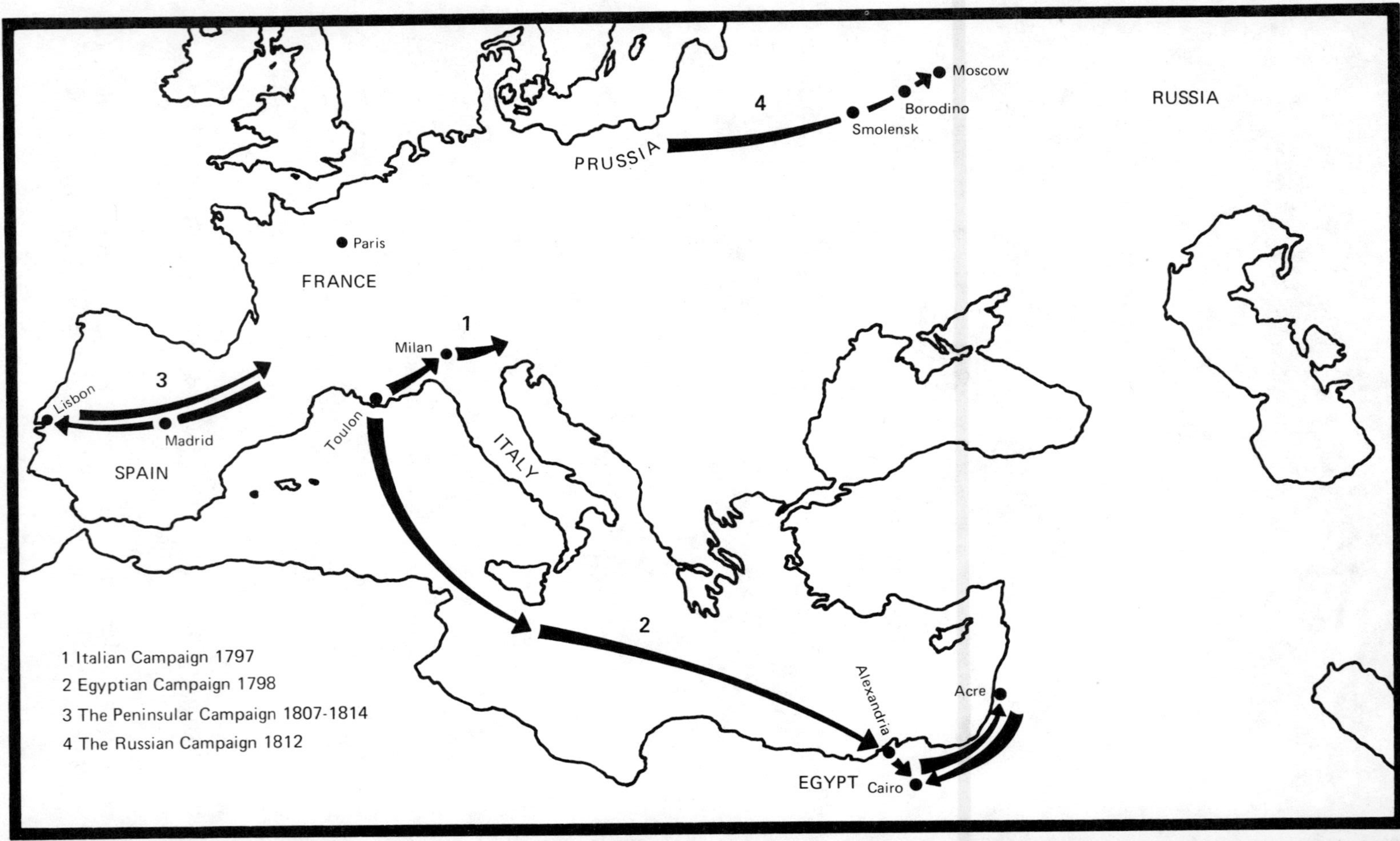
RUSSIA
Moscow
Borodino
Smolensk
4
PRUSSIA
Paris
FRANCE
1
Milan
3
Lisbon
Madrid
SPAIN
Toulon
ITALY
2
Alexandria
Acre
EGYPT
Cairo
1 Italian Campaign 1797
2 Egyptian Campaign 1798
3 The Peninsular Campaign 1807-1814
4 The Russian Campaign 1812

gone, Russia made a separate peace. In 1802 Britain also made peace, but war between Britain and France began again after little more than a year.

Napoleon's most important work while he was Consul was done inside France. He chose the men who were to serve his government according to how good they were at their jobs. He wanted clever men. It didn't matter whether they were former nobles or extreme revolutionaries so long as they were prepared to obey his orders. With their help he continued the reforms which the revolution had begun.

It was Napoleon who really established the modern system of local government in France. The Revolution had swept away the old muddle of local government. Instead, the country was divided up into roughly equal 'departments.' Until Napoleon came to power the new system did not work very well. He put new officials, called *prefects,* in charge of each department. They were highly trained and took all their orders from Napoleon in Paris. This policy of *centralization* made it possible for Napoleon to insist on other new reforms.

Before the Revolution the laws of France were a muddle. They were made up of ancient customs, the decrees of various kings and the decisions of courts. Sometimes one law contradicted another and it was difficult to find out just what the law was in any particular case. The revolutionaries had abolished some of the old laws and put new ones in their place. By the time Napoleon came to power the laws of France were more confused than ever. Napoleon knew that if a government expected the people to obey the law then the law must be clear and familiar to everyone. He therefore ordered a committee of lawyers to put all the laws together, cutting out those which were out of date or opposed to the new laws. The result was a collection of laws called the *'Code Napoleon'* and it has become a model for the reform of the law in many other countries. (D6) Napoleon himself said he was more proud of the Code than of all his victories. The Code upheld many of the liberal ideas of the Declaration of the Rights of Man *(The French Revolution)** – equal rights in law for everyone, legal guarantees of private property and freedom of worship. Freedom for groups of people to meet together and to criticize were, however, to be restricted by censorship and the use of spies and secret police. The Code also placed great importance on the family. (D7) Napoleon believed that a firm moral order was necessary to make people behave themselves.

For this same reason he reached an agreement with the Catholic Church. Napoleon recognised that Catholicism was 'the religion of the great majority of the citizens' of France. In return the Pope accepted the main parts of the revolutionary law which had put French priests under the control of the French government. Napoleon regarded this agreement as an important triumph, because it gave his government the support of an established church. The fact that the religion was Christianity did not matter to him, so long as

*Titles in brackets refer to other booklets in the Program

The Grand Coronation Procession of NAPOLEONE the

Garde d'Honneur', finishing the Procession.

Senator Fouché, Intendant General of ye Police, bearing the Sword of Justice

Bertheir, Bernadotte, Augerou & all the brave Train of Republican-Generals, marching in the Procession

Puissant Continental Powers, Train-Bearers to the Emperor.

Ladies of (cidevant, Poiss Train Bearers

The contemporary English view of Napoleon is shown in this cartoon of his coronation procession

The coronation of Napoleon by David. Napoleon takes the crown from the Pope and places it on his own head

it did not challenge his authority When he was in Egypt he pretended to be a Muslim. (D3) Later he said, 'If I were governin Jews, I should restore the temple of Solomon.'

By establishing his new Code laws and ending the quarrel between church and state, Napoleon satisfied the people's desire for order and won the support of the religious peasants for his government. He also pleased the business men by establishing a Bank of France rather like the Bank of England. This bank helped to handle government money, and lent money to traders and manufacturers.

In his reforms, Napoleon foun a balance between the new ideas of the revolution, the old traditions of the people and the

needs of the time. For this reason his reforms lasted. Napoleon was not democratic; he did not let the people decide how they would be governed. In 1802 he had himself elected First Consul for life. He stopped free discussion and would not allow anyone to oppose him. He allowed people to vote on important issues, but only when he was sure that they would support what he proposed. This did not seem to matter to the French people at that time. What they wanted was firm and efficient government and that was what Napoleon gave them.

from the Church of Notre Dame, Dec.r 2d 1804.
London. Publiſh'd Jan.y 1st 1805. by H. Humphrey 27 St James's Street.
Js Gillray inv.t & fec.t
His Holineſs Pope Pius VII, conducted by his old Faithful Friend; Cardinal Fesch, offering the Incense
Talleyrand-Perigord Prime Minister & King at Arms bearing the Emperor's Geneology.
Madame Talleyrand (ci devant Mrs Halhead the Propheteſs) conducting the Heir Apparent in ye Path of Glory.
The Three Imperial Graces, viz Their Imp. High. Princeſs Borghese, Princeſs Louis (cher amie of ye Emperor) & Princeſs Joseph-Bonaparte
His Imperial Highneſs Prince Louis Buonaparte Marboeuf High Conſtable of the Empire.

NAPOLEON THE EMPEROR: DOMINATING EUROPE.

In 1804 Napoleon, with great solemnity and in the presence of the Pope, crowned himself 'Emperor of the French'. This event was a turning point in his career. He had already shown himself to be ruthless and determined, but his actions had usually been for the good of France. After 1804 he acted more and more for the good of himself and to satisfy the greed of the Bonaparte family. The Emperor's crown was a symbol of privilege and harsh rule and was, therefore, an insult to the ideas of the Revolution. It represented many of the ideas the Revolution had attempted to destroy. (D8)

Napoleon seemed to go from strength to strength. His plan to invade England was stopped by Nelson's crushing naval victory at Trafalgar in 1805, but in the same year Napoleon won his greatest victory at Austerlitz, where he defeated the combined armies of Russia and Austria. In the following year he defeated the Prussians. Napoleon

The Battle of Trafalgar

was now free to re-draw the map of Europe and he did so.

Throughout the countries of Europe under Napoleon, the benefits of the revolution were introduced – feudalism and the rule of nobles were abolished: the Code Napoleon was introduced: restrictions against Jews were removed: weights, measures and currencies based on the decimal system replaced awkward traditional systems. The change helped trade. For a while the poorer people and the merchants and traders looked upon the French as liberators.

This feeling did not last. Napoleon's determination to destroy England, his most persistent enemy, led him to introduce the *Continental System.* This was an attempt to shut the whole of Europe off from trade with England. (D9) Napoleon hoped that this would choke England with goods she could not sell, and bring her to defeat by creating unemployment and commercial depression. But he was never able to prevent smuggling which enabled the English to reach some buyers in Europe. England also found new markets in South America and the East. But the Continental System had important effects in Europe, because everywhere business people were angered by Napoleon's interference with trade. Heavy war taxes, taking young men to serve in the French armies and the annoyance caused by being told what to do by their French ruler all helped to turn the 'liberated' peoples of Europe against Napoleon quite quickly. (D10) Napoleon later claimed that he had been trying to break down frontiers and make Europe one great civilised nation. (D11) In

Commerce overwhelms the blockade. A Cartoon of 1807

fact he started a nationalist reaction in which the inhabitants of Germany and Italy began for the first time to speak of themselves, not as Rhinelanders and Prussians, or Genovese and Romans, but as Germans and Italians. (D12) (On uniting Germany: *Bismarck) (Man and Nation)*

ıe French eagle crouching forms the hapeau en Militaire'
ıe Red Sea representing his throat is ıstrative of his drowning armies
ıe face is formed of carcases of the happy victims to his cruel ambition
ıe hand is judiciously placed as the aulet drawing the Rheinish confederacy der the flimsy symbol of the cobweb
ıe spider is a symbolic emblem of the ilance of the Allies

is German cartoon of 1813 shows how ıch Napoleon was hated

Y son fieras (And they are like wild beasts). *From the* Disasters of War *by Goya. This is one of the many pictures Goya drew to show the horrors of the guerilla fighting in the Peninsular War*

The changes brought by Napoleon's reforms did not only happen in areas directly under French power. In the Balkans contacts with the French increased as the Greek merchant fleet expanded to fill the place left by the British and French. Groups of merchants found the idea of good laws and efficient goverment attractive. They began to turn against the Ottoman rule. Revolution actually broke out in Serbia in 1804.

In Prussia, and in some other countries, reforms were carried through, but by men who hated France. They did this because they realized that the French administration and army were better than their own and in order to defeat France they would have to modernise their own states in the same way as France had done. Prussia, shamed by defeat and occupation by French troops, carried through a large number of reforms. The state bank was modernised, trade freed from old restrictions, local government improved and the serfs given personal freedom. All suitable men were ordered into the army and officers were chosen from all walks of life, not just from the nobles. Education and government service were also made to work better. The total effect of these changes was to make the Prussian state more efficient and to encourage the non-noble groups to take more part in its life. Thus

Napoleon's example in modern-ising France, helped to make the way for a strong united Germany.

In Britain, as a result of the wars, industry made great progress. The demand for arms led to the growth of her iron and engineering industries and the Continental System forced her merchants to seek out profitable new markets in Latin America and Asia. (D9)

The most fierce resistance to Napoleon arose in one of the most backward parts of Europe, Spain. In 1808 Napoleon put his brother Joseph on the throne of Spain and deposed the Spanish royal family. His main aim was to prevent Britain from finding a way into European markets through Spain. But the vast mass of Spanish peasants, who liked their monarchy and church, launched a fierce guerilla campaign against the French invaders, under the leader-ship of their priests and with the assistance of a British army under the Duke of Wellington. From 1809 onwards Napoleon, who desperately needed soldiers to fight in other parts of Europe, was forced to keep 250,000 troops in Spain fighting a war they could not win. (D13–14)

In 1809 the Austrians declared war on France again. Napoleon won a magnificent victory and as part of the peace settlement he married Marie Louise, the daughter of the Austrian Emperor. When his first son was born in 1811, the child was proclaimed King of Rome. Thereafter, Napoleon was determined to start a new royal family, a Napoleonic dynasty.

THE FALL OF THE EMPEROR

Napoleon's fall was finally made certain by his invasion of Russia. Both countries began to prepare for war and in June 1812 Napoleon invaded Russia. His Grand Army consisted of 600,000 troops, Only a small fraction of them were French. The Russians, with 200,000 men, retreated into the vast interior burning everything as they went to deprive the invaders of food for themselves and their horses. Desertions, deaths and disease reduced the Grand Army to half strength within six weeks, but Napoleon ignored the pleas of his generals to turn back before winter set in.

At Borodino the Russians at last turned to fight the French; victory

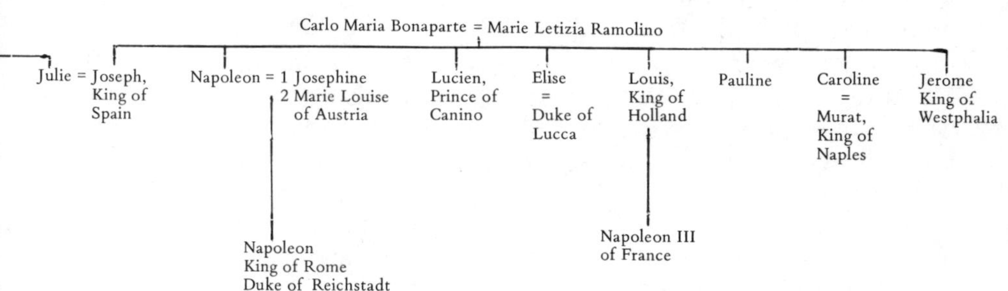

Napoleon's family tree

Cartoon of Napoleon's plans for founding a new European dynasty

cost Napoleon 30,000 dead. When he entered Moscow a week later he found the capital deserted. No one was there to surrender to him and the next day an unknown hand started a fire which destroyed half the city. It was a month before Napoleon realised that Russia could never be defeated. The country was too vast to be occupied and the people were fanatically loyal to the Tsar (emperor). On 19th October the long misery of the retreat from Moscow began. (D15) By the time Napoleon reached the German border only 30,000 men remained of his original army. (D16–17)

Once back in Paris Napoleon set about raising a fresh army, but he soon found himself faced by the most powerful alliance of all – England and Russia, his most persistant enemies, Austria, his former ally, Prussia and many lesser states had all united against him. He started fighting in the spring of 1813 and won one victory; then, however, he suffered the first major defeat of his career and was forced to abandon 60,000 men. He turned back to Paris. The Duke of Wellington came from Spain and advanced into France. The French, alarmed that fighting was taking place within their own country for the first time in 20 years, began to desert Napoleon in large numbers. They had had enough of taxes and war, and as allied troops approached Paris, Napoleon, deserted by his ministers and generals, gave up the throne he had made for himself.

The Allied powers then assembled at Vienna to plan the

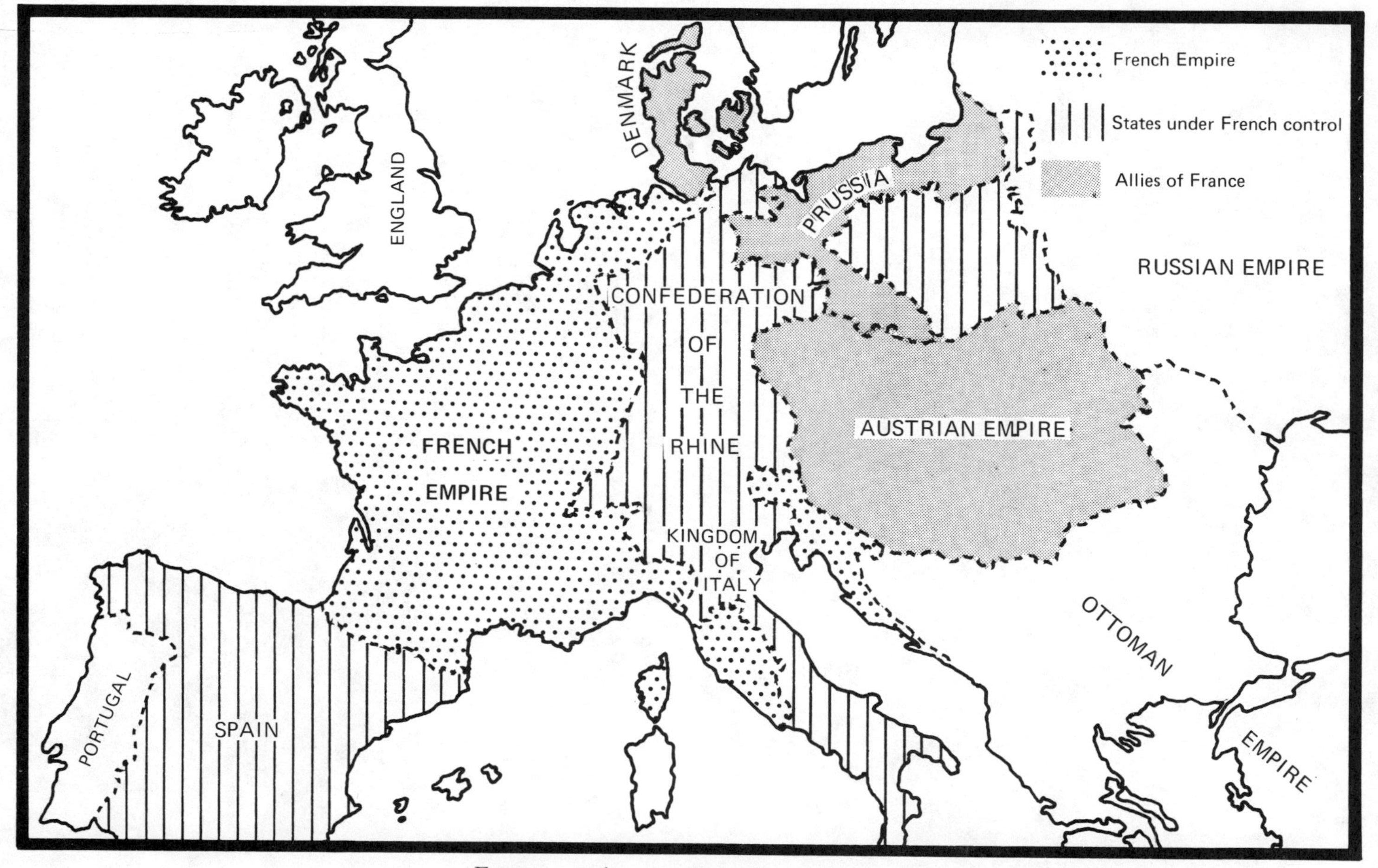

Europe under Napoleon – 1810

The retreat from Moscow. This picture shows vividly the misery of the long, bitterly cold march back to France

peace. Napoleon was exiled to the Mediterranean island of Elba, but he was not content to stay there. Ten months later he escaped back to France, where people flocke to cheer him. (D18) With a new army of 130,000 he was still supremely confident of his abili and luck. 'I tell you that Wellington is a bad general,' he declared, 'that the English are b troops and that it will be a picn In fact the battle of Waterloo in Belgium was a close fought and bitter fight, which the French o just lost. 'The most desperate business I ever was in and never was so near being beat', Welling confessed afterwards. Waterloo the end for Napoleon. The Briti sent him to the bleak Atlantic island of St Helena. He remaine there, with a small group of fait ful followers, until he died in 18

Cartoon of Napoleon (shown as an ape from the waist down) being attacked by the Russian bear and the British bulldog

AFTER NAPOLEON IN EURO

Faced with re-drawing the frontiers of Europe, the victorio countries wanted to make sure that no one country should ever be able to dominate Europe agai The growing feelings of nationalism in many parts of

Napoleon being welcomed by the French on his return from Elba

Europe were ignored, and many of the kings and countries swept away by Napoleon were restored.

France kept much of her power, although she lost almost all the territory she had gained by war in

The Battle of Waterloo. This was the final defeat for Napoleon

Napoleon on his way to exile in St Helena

the previous twenty years and was forced to suffer an army of occupation and to pay large sums of money. Along her frontiers there stretched powerful new states. Prussia and Russia were enlarged. Britain gained most from the years of war, acquiring many overseas possessions.

AFTER NAPOLEON IN FRANCE

Napoleon changed France in many ways. His new code of laws, his educational reforms and his system of administration survive today. But his constant warfare made France a weaker country for a long time. He was a brilliant administrator and general, and a remarkable man. He rose to power on the strength of his own talents during wartime. For fifteen years he was the dominant figure in Europe and his fall was caused as much by the failure of his own power as by the fact that his enemies had at last united.

NAPOLEON AND THE WORLD

Napoleon's career had very important effects on the history of North and South America. The territory of the United States was enlarged by the sale to the American government of the former French possessions on the American mainland, stretching north from New Orleans along the Mississippi to Ohio. This sale, known as the Louisiana Purchase, was completed in 1803. (D19)

Haiti, formerly a French colony in the West Indies, won its independence during this period. Inspired by the ideas of the French revolution, which proclaimed the equality of all men, the black slaves rose in revolt. *(The Slave Trade)* They defeated an army which Napoleon sent to restore order, although their leader, Toussaint l'Ouverture, was captured and died in prison in France. (D20)

Napoleon's invasion of Spain led

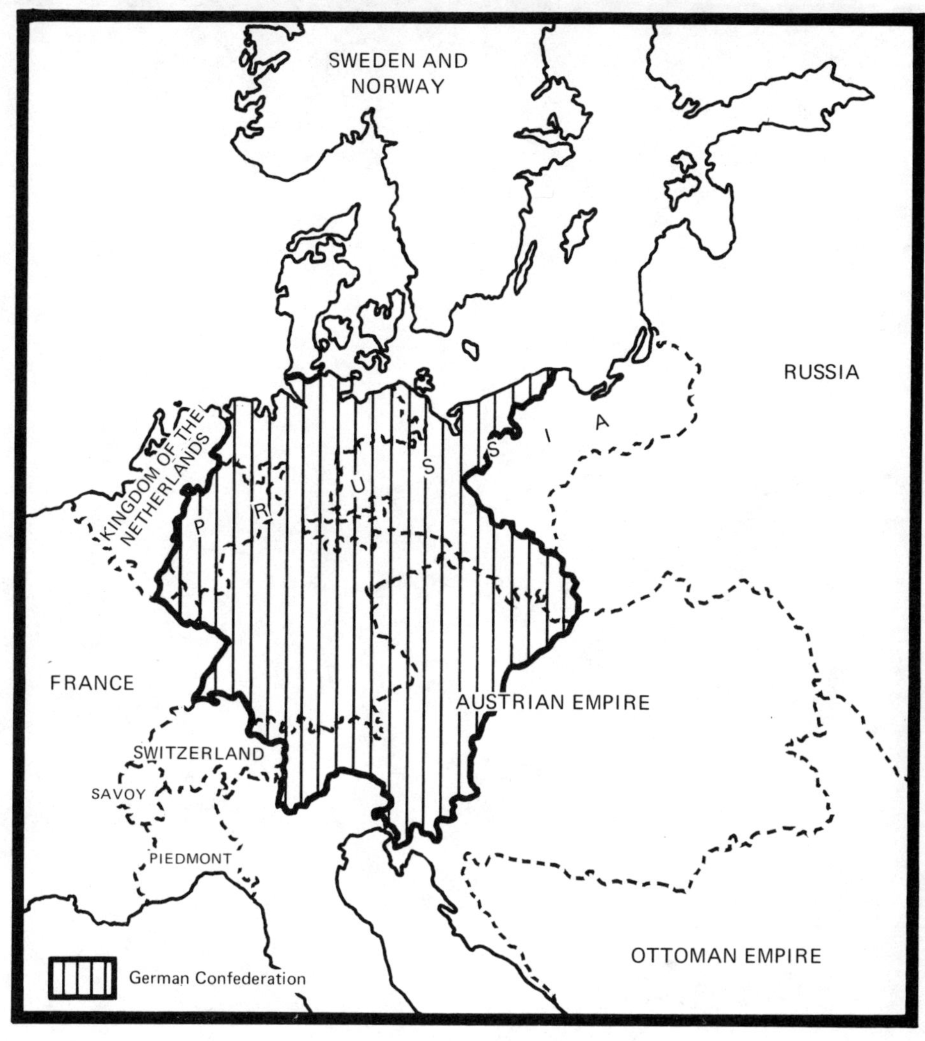

Europe after Napoleon. Treaty of Vienna, 1815

to the break-up of the Spanish empire in South America. By 1810 most of the former Spanish colonies were in revolt. Led by Bolivar and San Martin, they managed to achieve their independence by the 1820s. *(Bolivar)* Napoleon's invasion also led the Portuguese royal family to flee to Brazil, a Portuguese colony. They returned from exile in 1815, but the heir to the throne stayed in Brazil and led the country to independence in 1822. He became Emperor Pedro I of Brazil.

Because Napoleon tried to stop Britain from trading with Europe, British merchants began to trade with South America. This led the British government to support independence movements.

Napoleon also became very interested in the Middle East and North Africa. The expedition which led to Egypt in 1798 was just the beginning. At different times he

Napoleon and the Americas

made alliances with the Ottoman Empire and Iran, and French soldiers were sent to train their armies. French agents went to many countries in the area. Two things happened as a result. One was that the countries of the Middle East came to like French ways and try to copy them in the future. (D21) The other was that Britain did not like these French agents coming so near to her lands in India. So British soldiers and agents were also sent to the Middle East. This was the beginning of a long story of European rivalry in the Middle East.

THE IDEA OF NAPOLEON

Napoleon is an important man in world history not just because of what he did in France and the rest of the world, but because of the effect he had on men's sense of their own power and capabilities. Before his time people's ideas of what was possible were much more limited; they thought in small terms. Napoleon thought big, and to many men it seemed that he could do almost anything. (D11) They thought he could make a better world. Although Napoleon's world ended in misery the idea was not lost and in the future men were to look for new Napoleons. Napoleon was the first modern dictator. We have seen many other dictators like Hitler and Stalin and what evil they can do. But it is important to understand why they find so many people to follow them and looking at Napoleon's career helps us to understand that.

DOCUMENT 1

PROCLAMATIONS TO THE ARMY OF ITALY *NAPOLEON –*

From General Headquarters. Nice. 7 Germinal Year IV (March 27, 1796)

Soldiers you are naked, ill-fed; the Government owes you much; it can give you nothing. Your patience and the courage, which you have shown in the midst of these crags, are admirable; but they have won you no glory; no glamour clings about you. I wish to lead you into the most fertile plains in the world. Rich provinces, great cities will be in your power; you will find honour, glory and riches there. Soldiers of Italy; do you lack courage or constancy?

From Headquarters at Cherasco. 7 Floréal Year IV (April 26, 1796)

Soldiers: In fifteen days you have won six victories, taken twenty-one standards, fifty-five pieces of artillery, many fortified places, and conquered the richest part of Piedmont; you have made fifteen thousand prisoners and killed or wounded more than ten thousand men.

Until now you have fought for barren rocks made famous by your courage but useless to the fatherland; now your services place you on a level with the armies of Holland and of the Rhine. Without supplies you have supplied everything. Without cannon you have won battles; without bridges you have crossed rivers; without shoes you have made forced marches . . . Only republican ranks, soldiers of liberty, are capable of enduring what you have suffered. Thanks should be given to you soldiers! Your country will owe its prosperity to you . . .

DOCUMENT 2

PROCLAMATION TO THE ARMY IN EGYPT *NAPOLEON – From his headquarters on board the ship* L'Orient *in 1798*

Soldiers, you are going to carry out a conquest, the effects of which upon the civilization and commerce of the world are beyond all calculation.

You will give England the most definite and palpable blow that could be given, pending the day when you are able to give her the death-blow.

We shall make some tiring marches; we shall be engaged in several battles; but we shall succeed in all that we undertake, for destiny is on our side.

The people amongst whom you are going to live will be Mohammedans; the first article of their faith is that 'There is no other God save God and Mohammed is his prophet.'

Do not contradict them; treat them as we treated the Jews or the Italians; pay due respect to their *muftis* and *imams,* as you did to the rabbis and bishops.

Show the same toleration to the mosques and to the ceremonies prescribed in the Koran, as you showed to the convents and synagogues, to the religions of Moses and Jesus Christ.

You will find that the customs here are different from those of Europe; however, you must get used to them.

The people amongst whom you are going to live do not treat women as we treat them; but in all countries he who violates is a monster.

Plundering only enriches a small number of men; it dishonours us, and destroys our resources, and it makes us enemies of the people whom it is our interest to have as friends.

DOCUMENT 3

NAPOLEON'S ADDRESS TO THE PEOPLE OF EGYPT

In the name of God, the Merciful and Compassionate; there is no God but God;

In the name of the French Republic, based upon the foundations of Liberty and Equality, Bonaparte, the Commander-in-Chief of the French Forces, informs all the population of Egypt:

For a long time, those in power in Egypt have insulted the French Nation and unfairly treated her merchants by various deceitful and aggressive tactics. Now, the hour of their punishment has arrived.

People of Egypt, some may say to you that I do not come except to destroy your religion. That is an outright lie; do not believe it. Tell those liars that I came only to rescue your rights from the oppressors. And that I worship Almighty God and respect his Prophet Muhammad and the glorious Koran more than the Mamluks do. Tell them also that all people are equal before God. . . .

With God's help, from now on, no Egyptian will be barred from entering the highest positions and from reaching the highest rank. The intelligent, virtuous and learned men will take charge of affairs and thus the condition of the entire nation will improve.

Formerly there were great cities, wide canals and thriving commerce in Egypt, all of which have disappeared as a result of the Mamluks' greed and oppression.

The French at every time have been the most faithful friend of the Ottoman Sultan and the enemy of his enemies, may God preserve his reign, and destroy the Mamluks who refused to obey him and heed his orders. . . .

Blessings and happiness to the Egyptian people who support us from the first. . . . But woe to those who join the Mamluks and aid them in the war against us; they will find no way to escape and no trace of them will be left.

DOCUMENT 4

NAPOLEON *A description in 1802*

He is about five feet seven inches high, delicately and gracefully made; his hair a dark brown crop, thin and lank; his complexion smooth, pale and sallow; his eyes grey, but very animated, his eyebrows light brown, thin and projecting. All his features, particularly his mouth and nose, fine, sharp, defined and expressive beyond description. The free expression of his countenance is a pleasing melancholy, which, whenever he speaks, relaxes into the most agreeable and gracious smile you can conceive.

DOCUMENT 5

NAPOLEON *A description in 1807*

He is excessively ugly, with a fat swollen sallow face, very corpulent, besides short and entirely without figure. His great eyes roll gloomily around; the expression of his features is severe; he looks like the incarnation of fate; only his mouth is well shaped, and his teeth are good.

DOCUMENT 6

THE CODE NAPOLEON *PORTALIS – The State Counsellor explaining the advantages of the new code of laws in a speech made in 1804*

To-day uniform laws will remove all absurdities and dangers; civil order will cement political order. We will no longer be provençals, Bretons or Alsacians, but only Frenchmen. Names have a greater influence than one believes on men's thoughts and actions. . . .

Formerly humiliating distinctions which political privilege had introduced among persons had also invaded civil rights. There was a law of succession for nobles, and another for those who were not. . . All these traces of barbarism have been removed; the law is the common mother of all citizens; she gives equal protection to all. One of the great achievements of the new code is also to have brought to an end all civil differences between men who profess different beliefs. Religious opinions are free. The law no longer seeks to force consciences. . . .

There has been no attempt to introduce dangerous novelties into the new legislation. All has been preserved from the old laws which can be reconciled with the present order of society; the stability of marriage has been upheld; wise rules for the government of families have been provided; the authority of fathers has been re-established; . . . . care has been given to the maintenance of good customs, the reasonable freedom of trade and every object which concerns civil society. . . .

DOCUMENT 7

THE EDUCATION OF WOMAN *NAPOLEON*

We must begin with religion in all its severity. Do not admit any modification of this. Religion is very important in a girl's public school. It is the surest guarantee for mothers and husbands. We must train up believers, not reasoners. The weakness of women's brains, their need of constant resignation and of a kind of indulgent and easy charity – all can only be attained by religion.

DOCUMENT 8

THE NAPOLEONIC CATECHISM OF 1806

All French children had to learn this.

Question: What are the duties of Christians with reference to their governing princes, and what in particular are our duties toward Napoleon I, our Emperor?
Answer: Christians owe to the princes who govern them, and we owe in particular to our Emperor, Napoleon I, love, respect, obedience, fidelity, military service, and the taxes levied for the preservation and defence of the empire and of his throne. We also owe him ferevent prayers for his safety and for the spiritual and temporal prosperity of the state.
Q.: Why are we held to all these duties toward our Emperor?
A.: First, because God, who has created empires and distributed them according to His will, has, be blessing our Emperor with gifts in both peace and war, established him as our sovereign and made him the agent of His power and His image upon earth. To honour and to serve our Emperor is, the, to honour and to serve God Himself. . . .
Q: Are there not particular motives which should attach us more closely to Napoleon I, our Emperor?
A: Yes. For it is he whom God has raised up in trying times to re-establish the public worship of the holy religion of our fathers and to be its protector. He has restored and preserved public order by his profound and active wisdom; he defends the state by his mighty arm; he has become the anointed of the Lord by the consecration which he received from the sovereign pontiff, head of the Universal Church.

DOCUMENT 9

THE BRITISH ECONOMY AND THE CONTINENTAL SYSTEM

SCOTTISH COTTON MASTER – writing in 1812

In 1808 trade revived considerably; a great quantity of our goods was introduced into the Continent through Heligoland. A very great trade was open to this country in consequence of the Royal Family of Portugal removing to Brazil, which likewise made an opening to Spanish South America. . . . The trade of this country, in the years 1808 and 1809 until the spring of 1810 increased very considerably. We attribute the depression which took place in 1810 to the effect of the Berlin and Milan decrees. After the spring of 1810 the whole of the northern coast from

Holland to the Elbe was completely shut against us. It was the same with all the lower part of the Baltic.

DOCUMENT 10

SUPPRESSING FREE SPEECH *NAPOLEON – Writing to Marshall Bertier in Germany in 1806.*

I imagine that you have arrested the Augsberg and Nuremberg booksellers. My intention is to bring them before a court-martial and to have them shot within twenty-four hours. It is no ordinary crime to spread defamatory writings in places occupied by the French armies and to incite the inhabitants against them. It is high treason. The sentence must declare that, since wherever an army may be, it is the duty of its commander to see to its safety, such and such individuals, having been found guilty of trying to rouse the inhabitants of Swabia against the French army, are condemned to death. You are to have the sentence published all over Germany.

DOCUMENT 11

A UNITED EUROPE *NAPOLEON – writing of the plans he had for Europe in his memoirs dictated on St Helena between 1815 and 1821*

Peace, concluded at Moscow, would have fulfilled and wound up my hostile expeditions. A new horizon, new undertakings, would have unfolded themselves, adapted in every respect to the well-being and prosperity of all. The foundation of the European system would have been laid and my only remaining task would have been its organisation.

The cause of the Revolution was victorious – the only question was to reconcile it with what it had not destroyed. I became the arch of the old and new alliance, the natural mediator between the ancient and modern order of things. I maintained the principles and possessed the confidence of the one; I had identified myself with the other. I belonged to them both; I should have acted conscientiously in favour of each.

I would have sought the prosperity, the interests, the enjoyments and the well-being of the European confederacy; established the same principles, the same system everywhere; a European code; a court of European appeal with full powers to redress all wrong decisions; money of the same value but with different coins; the same weights; the same measures; the same laws, etc.

I would have required that all the rivers should be navigable in common; that the seas should be thrown open; that the great standing armies should in future, be reduced to the single establishment of a guard for the sovereign, etc.

On my return to France, in the bosom of my country, at once great, powerful, magnificent, at peace and glorious, I would have proclaimed the immutability of boundaries; all future wars purely defensive; all new aggrandizement anti-national. I would have associated my son with the empire; my dictatorship would have terminated, and his constitutional reign have commenced. . . Paris would have been the capital of the world and the French the envy of nations. . . These also were among my dreams.

DOCUMENT 12

PRUSSIAN NATIONALISM *FREDERICK WILLIAM III – The King of Prussia calls for a rising against the French invader in 1812*

There is no need of explaining to my loyal subjects, or to any German, the reasons for the war which is about to begin. They lie plainly before the eyes of awakened Europe. We succumbed to the superior force of France. The peace which followed deprived me of my people and, far from bringing us blessings, it inflicted upon us deeper wounds than the war itself, sucking out the very marrow of the country. Our principal fortresses remained in the hands of the enemy, and agriculture, as well as the highly developed industries of our towns, was crippled. The freedom of trade was hampered, and thereby the sources of commerce and prosperity cut off. . . .

Brandenburgers, Prussians, Silesians, Pomeranians, Lithuanians! You know what you have borne for the last seven years; you know the sad fate that awaits you if we do not bring this war to an honourable end. Think of the past – of the Great Elector, the great Frederick! Remember the blessings for which your forefathers fought under their leadership and which they paid for with their blood – freedom of conscience, national honour, independence, commerce, industry, learning. Look at the great example of our powerful allies, the Russians; look at the Spaniards, the Portuguese. For such objects as these even weaker peoples have gone forth against mightier enemies and returned in triumph. Witness the heroic Swiss and the people of the Netherlands. . .

This is the final, the decisive struggle; upon it depends our independence, our prosperity, our existence. There are no other alternatives but an honourable peace or a heroic end. You would willingly face even the latter for honour's sake, for without honour no Prussian or German could live.

DOCUMENT 13

THE WAR IN SPAIN *A Swiss soldier with the French armies recalls the beginning of the campaign*

Not a Frenchman then doubted that such rapid victories must have decided the fate of the Spaniards. We believed, and Europe believed it too, that we had only to march to Madrid to complete the subjection of Spain and to organise the country in the French manner, that is to say, to increase our means of conquest by all the resources of our vanquished enemies. The wars we had hitherto carried on had accustomed us to see in a nation only its military forces and to count for nothing the spirit which animates its citizens.

DOCUMENT 14

THE WAR IN SPAIN *Extracts from a letter written home by a French soldier later in the campaign*

Dear Mother, I don't think that since the day I became a soldier I have ever been so badly off as now. For the past month and a half we have been in the mountains, chasing guerillas. All these mountains have been pillaged in such a manner that there is not one soul that is not against us. We never find peasants in the villages here, so that we are the only inhabitants. The peasants are all bandits. Every day they murder some of our men. We burn their villages. But it is all in vain. They are terrible people. From the youngest to the oldest they are all our enemies.

DOCUMENT 15

THE RETREAT FROM MOSCOW *NAPOLEON – Writing from Doubrovna, 18 November, 1812*

. . . . Since my last despatch, our position has grown worse. Almost all of our horses – 30,000 of them – have perished as the result of the cold – 16 degrees of frost. The cold weather has greatly increased the number of stragglers. The Cossacks have taken advantage of our complete lack of cavalry, and almost complete lack of artillery, to harass us and to cut our communications, so that I am anxious about Marshal Ney, who stayed behind with 3,000 men to blow up Smolensk. Otherwise, given a few days' rest, some good food, (above all) horses, and a supply of artillery, we shall still make good. . . .

DOCUMENT 16

THE RETREAT FROM MOSCOW *SIR ROBERT THOMAS WILSON – An English soldier and diplomat who fought with the Russians, describing the retreat in his diary*

Every day since we have been here, prisoners in parties of fifty, and even of a hundred, have been brought in, chiefly wounded. During the five days that we remained at Krasnoi Pakra, thirteen hundred and forty-two were delivered to the commandant at head-quarters. Of course many more are killed; for such is the inveteracy of the peasants that they buy prisoners off the Cossacks for several roubles to put them to death.

The baggage taken is enormous, and its value immense. One waggon was full of gold and silver ingots. Another military chest had two hundred thousand pounds. Davoust's carriage had his Marhsal's staff, all his insignia, private correspondence, the French ciphers, manuscript maps, etc.

For the last two months, I have seen very nearly as many dead and dying as living beings. The enemy have a disease internally, occasioned by eating horse-flesh without bread and salt, that carries off nine-tenths even of those who survive the field and epidemic sickness. Change of diet causes almost instant death. The dead, however, are to be envied. With frost to twenty-eight and thirty degrees, all prisoners are immediately and invariably stripped stark naked and marched in columns in that state, or turned adrift to be the sport and victims of the peasantry.

DOCUMENT 17

THE RETREAT FROM MOSCOW *FRENCH COMMANDER – reporting on his losses during the retreat*

Imperial Guard. 6th Light Infantry Regiment.
1st Division. Situation on 19 December 1812.

Lost since the departure from Smolensk

Present under arms at the departure from Smolensk		Killed in Action		Wounded who were left behind in the hands of the enemy		Dead from cold or starvation		Left behind from frostbite and sickness in the hands of the enemy		Total losses		Now present under arms	
Offrs	Ptes	Offrs	Ptes	Offrs	Ptes	Offrs	Ptes	Offrs	Ptes	Offrs	Ptes	Offrs	Ptes
31	300	-	13	4	52	-	24	13	201	17	290	14	10

Signed. Carre. Lt. Col. commanding the above regiment.

The other regiments are more or less in the same state.

DOCUMENT 18

DECLARATION OF THE POWERS AGAINST NAPOLEON: 1815

The Powers who have signed the Treaty of Paris, reassembled in Congress at Vienna, having been informed of the escape of Napoleon Bonaparte and of his entrance into France with an armed force, owe to their dignity and the interest of social order a solemn Declaration of the sentiments which that event has inspired in them.

In thus violating the convention which established him in the Island of Elba, Bonoparte destroyed the only legal title for his existence. By reappearing in France with projects of disorder and destruction, he has cut himself off from the protection of the law and has shown in the face of the world that there can be neither peace nor truce with him.

Accordingly, the Powers declare that Napoleon Bonoparte is excluded from civil and social relations, and, as an Enemy and Disturber of the tranquillity of the World, that he has incurred public vengeance.

At the same time, being firmly resolved to preserve intact the Treaty of Paris of May 30, 1814, and the arrangements sanctioned by that treaty, they declare that they will employ all their resources and will unite all their efforts in order that the General Peace, the object of the desires of Europe and the constant aim of their labours, may not be again disturbed, and in order to secure themselves from all attempts which may threaten to plunge the World once more into the disorders and misfortunes of revolutions.

DOCUMENT 19

THE LOUISIANA PURCHASE *NAPOLEON – Writing about the Purchase on 11 April, 1802*

Irresolution and deliberation are no longer in season. I renounce Louisiana. It is not only New Orleans that I cede: it is the whole colony, without reserve; I know the price of what I abandon. I have proved the importance I attach to this province since my first diplomatic cut with Spain had the object of recovering it. I renounce it with the utmost regret; to attempt obstinately to retain it would be folly.

DOCUMENT 20

HAITI'S INDEPENDENCE *TOUSSAINT L'OUVERTURE – From a letter addressed to Napoleon in 1801*

You say in your letter that Haiti is showing a tendency to independence. Why should this not be so? The United States of America did exactly that; and with the assistance of France, succeeded. The high post which I hold has been as legitimately acquired as your own, and nothing but the expressed wish of the people of Haiti will force me to give it up.

DOCUMENT 21

THE FRENCH IN EGYPT *EL-DJABARTI – An Arab writer who attended the Institute of Egypt, set up by Napoleon*

The French installed a great library, with several librarians. The readers assembled in a large room next to the one where the books were kept. They sat down in chairs around large tables and started to work. When a Moslem wished to visit the establishment, he was not prevented from doing so, but on the contrary, was made very welcome. The French were particularly pleased when a Moslem visitor showed interest in the sciences. In the observatory there were instruments remarkable for their great precision. There also were telescopes that could be disassembled and packed into small boxes. When an animal or a fish unknown in France was discovered, it was placed in a liquid which preserved it indefinitely.

We were shown a machine in which a glass was rotating; at the approach of a foreign body, the glass emitted sparks and produced a crackling sound. If a person held in his hand an object, even a mere wire, and touched the rotating glass with it, his body instantly received a shock that made the bones in his shoulders and arms crack. . . We were shown other experiments as well, all as extraordinary as the first ones, such as intelligences like ours can neither conceive of nor explain.

He also watched some of the road building and other works started by the French

The workers were paid generous wages – much more than they were used to; they received their pay every day in the afternoon. They were given highly improved and simple tools. Thus, instead of baskets and jars, they used little carts with two handles, which the workingmen filled with dirt or stones, and then pushed on a wheel. Each wheelbarrow had a capacity of five baskets. The labourers filled, moved and emptied these wheelbarrows with the greatest ease.

ACKNOWLEDGMENTS

Radio Times Hulton Picture Library pages 2, 4 top, 8 bottom, 10, 12, 16 (both pictures), 17 bottom; the Mansell Collection pages 4 bottom, 5, 8 top, 9, 11 bottom, 14, 17 top, 18; John Freeman and Co. Ltd page 11 top.

Greenhaven World History Program

History Makers
Alexander
Constantine
Leonardo Da Vinci
Columbus
Luther, Erasmus and Loyola
Napoleon
Bolivar
Adam Smith, Malthus and Marx
Darwin
Bismark
Henry Ford
Roosevelt
Stalin
Mao Tse-Tung
Gandhi
Nyerere and Nkrumah

Great Civilizations
The Ancient Near East
Ancient Greece
Pax Romana
The Middle Ages
Spices and Civilization
Chingis Khan and the Mongol Empire
Akbar and the Mughal Empire
Traditional China
Ancient America
Traditional Africa
Asoka and Indian Civilization
Mohammad and the Arab Empire
Ibin Sina and the Muslim World
Suleyman and the Ottoman Empire

Great Revolutions
The Neolithic Revolution
The Agricultural Revolution
The Scientific Revolution
The Industrial Revolution
The Communications Revolution
The American Revolution
The French Revolution
The Mexican Revolution
The Russian Revolution
The Chinese Revolution

Enduring Issues
Cities
Population
Health and Wealth
A World Economy
Law
Religion
Language
Education
The Family

Political and Social Movements
The Slave Trade
The Enlightenment
Imperialism
Nationalism
The British Raj and Indian Nationalism
The Growth of the State
The Suez Canal
The American Frontier
Japan's Modernization
Hitler's Reich
The Two World Wars
The Atom Bomb
The Cold War
The Wealth of Japan
Hollywood